Facilitator's Guide

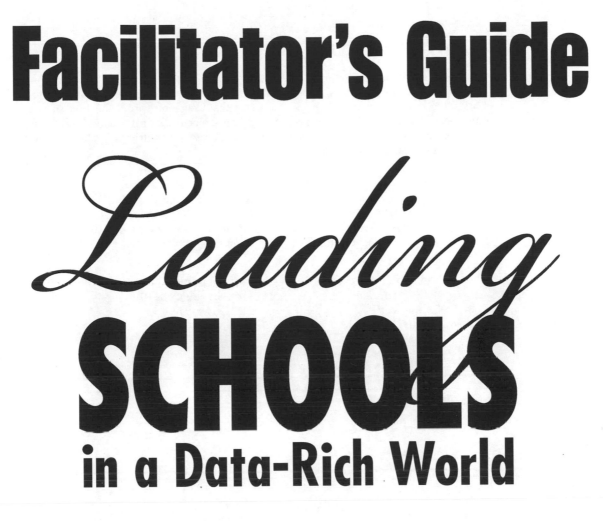

Leading

SCHOOLS
in a Data-Rich World

Harnessing Data for School Improvement

LORNA M. EARL
STEVEN KATZ
SONIA BEN JAAFAR

CORWIN PRESS
A SAGE Publications Company
Thousand Oaks, CA 91320

Copyright © 2008 by Corwin Press.

For information:

Corwin Press
A Sage Publications Company
2455 Teller Road
Thousand Oaks, California 91320
www.corwinpress.com

Sage Publications Ltd.
1 Oliver's Yard
55 City Road
London EC1Y 1SP
United Kingdom

Sage Publications India Pvt. Ltd.
B 1/I 1 Mohan Cooperative Industrial Area
Mathura Road, New Delhi 110 044
India

Sage Publications Asia-Pacific Pte. Ltd.
33 Pekin Street #02-01
Far East Square
Singapore 048763

Printed in the United States of America

ISBN 978-1-4129-5512-6

This book is printed on acid-free paper.

07 08 09 10 11 10 9 8 7 6 5 4 3 2 1

Acquisitions Editor:	Debra Stollenwerk
Editorial Assistant:	Jordan Barbakow
Production Editor:	Melanie Birdsall
Copy Editor:	Kristin Bergstad
Typesetter:	C&M Digitals (P) Ltd.
Proofreader:	Charlotte J. Waisner
Cover Designer:	Michael Dubowe

Contents

About the Authors

Lorna M. Earl is Director, Aporia Consulting, Ltd., and a recently retired Associate Professor in the Theory and Policy Studies Department and Head of the International Centre for Educational Change at the Ontario Institute for Studies in Education at the University of Toronto (OISE/UT). Her career has spanned research, policy, and practice in school districts, provincial government, and academe. After twenty-five years as a Research Officer and Research Director in school districts, she was the first Director of Assessment for the Ontario Education Quality and Accountability Office. Dr. Earl is a teacher and researcher with a background in psychology and education and a doctorate in Epidemiology and Biostatistics. As a leader in the field of assessment and evaluation, she has been involved in consultation, research, and staff development with teachers' organizations, ministries of education, school boards, and charitable foundations around the world.

Steven Katz is a director with the research and evaluation firm Aporia Consulting, Ltd. and a faculty member in Human Development and Applied Psychology at the Ontario Institute for Studies in Education (OISE) of the University of Toronto. He is an associate member of the School of Graduate Studies and is the coordinator of the Psychology of Learning and Development initial teacher education strand.

Dr. Katz holds a doctorate in human development and applied psychology, with a specialization in cognitive science. His areas of expertise include cognition and learning, teacher education, and the design of data-driven systems for organizational accountability, planning, and improvement. He has received the Governor General's medal for excellence in his field and has been involved in research and evaluation, professional development, and consulting with a host of educational organizations around the world.

Sonia Ben Jaafar is a Research Associate at Aporia Consulting, Ltd. Her consulting work supports policy and program development and implementation through applied research and evaluation. She helps educators and educational leaders understand the nature of data in their context, and how they can be used for various purposes.

She graduated from the Ontario Institute for Studies in Education of the University of Toronto with a PhD in Theory and Policy Studies. Her research focuses on how assessment and accountability policies influence school practices. She also holds an MA in Curriculum, Teaching and Learning, a BEd from the University of British Columbia, and a BSc in Biochemistry.

Her work experiences include supporting applied research and evaluation in several boards in Ontario. She supported program evaluations for the departments of pharmacy at the University of Toronto, British Columbia, and Ottawa. She was the project manager in charge of developing the PRIME diagnostic tests.

When she works with educators, in addition to drawing on her research and evaluation knowledge, she draws from her experience as a mathematics teacher and Science Department Chair. She hopes that this facilitator's guide will help school leaders build capacity for evidence-informed decision making in their schools.

Introduction

Facilitators who are working with schools to build capacity for leading in a data-rich world need to be knowledgeable about and sensitive to the change process required to support new learning and the shift in school culture to sustain the inquiry process, as well as having an understanding of data, data analysis, and data interpretation. This *Facilitator's Guide* offers activities for facilitators to use to support educators in the thinking work needed to move forward in using data to improve schools. Although the *Facilitator's Guide* can be used as supportive study material, it primarily provides directions, suggestions, activities, and guiding questions for facilitators to practically engage a group in the process of collaborative inquiry within their local context, using data that is directly relevant to them.

This *Facilitator's Guide* is designed to provide support to facilitators who are working with schools in studying and applying the concepts included in the book *Leading Schools in a Data-Rich World: Harnessing Data for School Improvement*. This guide is organized to parallel the chapters in the book, giving the facilitator ideas, suggestions, and tasks that she or he can use in guiding the group through the materials and helping them go deeper in their use of data for improvement in their schools. It is organized in seven segments that vary from a few hours to multiple days in length. Suggested times are posted on each segment. Each segment is organized in a similar format:

- *Notes for Facilitators* that highlight the key ideas that the facilitator should pay attention to while introducing and guiding the different sections.

- *Discussion Questions* that can be used to engage participants meaningfully in the work and help relate it back to their contexts.
- *Activities* that the facilitator can use to engage the group in working with the ideas and work with them given their own school situations.

It is important for a facilitator who is about to lead a team through this process to read through the entire guide before proceeding. The facilitator needs to understand the direction of the process, the range of activities that are presented in the guide, how the thinking products from one activity are connected to the subsequent phases, and how these products will be used in future activities. This is especially important because the format of the guide is linear, but the process is iterative. Each activity will result in a product or learning that represents the collaborative thinking of the group at a given point in the process that must be connected to other processes and decisions. Hence, the facilitator needs to be familiar with the whole process to be able to move through the activities and revisit thinking products as more clarity develops in subsequent phases.

Finally, it is important to recognize the time that is required to complete the process. The book and guide provide a supportive framework for leaders to guide a school (or district) through a process that requires time to think, reflect, prioritize, collect and analyze information, and make intelligent decisions. The series of activities in this guide and in the book should take a few months to complete.

Suggested Timeline for Workshop Schedule

Activities can be recast into a workshop series that meets the needs of the group to engage with the work rather than the chapter. This type of organization promotes continuity in the flow of work over time and supports the iterative process of using data for school improvement. The table on pages 3 and 4 of this guide presents a suggested grouping of activities by segment for a workshop series over the time allotted. We believe that the process will take from six to nine months to complete. Segments can be grouped together at the discretion of the facilitator to suit the scheduling of the workshops. It is important for the participants to have time to reflect and work with their planning and their data along the way as well.

Segment	Activities	Time	Materials
Segment 1: What Do You Believe About Your School? (Chapter 1) *Approximately 2 hours*	Describe the Context of Your School	45–50 minutes	Paper and pen
	Beliefs About Accountability	45 minutes	Copies of Task Sheet #2 (pages 111–112), chart paper, masking tape, and markers
	Collective Beliefs About Accountability With Purpose	30 minutes	Copies of Task Sheet #2 (pages 111–112), chart paper, masking tape, and markers
Segment 2: Capacities for Using Data for Decision Making (Chapters 2 and 3) *Approximately 3 hours*	Self-Assessment of Capacities for Learning in a Data-Rich World	10–15 minutes	Copies of Task Sheet #3 (page 113)
	Capacities for Leading in a Data-Rich World	90 minutes	Copies of Task Sheet #3 (page 113), notepads, pens
	Building a Culture of Inquiry in the School Community	30 minutes	Chart paper
	Painting a Data-Rich Picture	20–30 minutes	Copies of the Metaphor Reflection Activity Sheet (Handout 1) and pens
Segment 3: What Is the Context and Direction of This Inquiry? (Chapter 4) *Approximately 6 hours*	Purpose, Context, and Roles	30–40 minutes	Copies of Task Sheet #4 (page 114), index cards, scissors, and pens
	Identifying Audiences	30–40 minutes	Copies of Task Sheet #5 (page 115), markers, pens, two different colors of sticky notes, chart paper, and masking tape
	Possible Futures	80–90 minutes	Copies of Task Sheet #6 (page 116), chart paper, markers, masking tape, and sticky notes
	Probable Futures	30–40 minutes	Copies of Task Sheet #6 (page 116), possible futures concept map, chart paper, blank paper, pens, and markers
	Preferable Futures	35–45 minutes	Copies of Task Sheet #6 (page 116), possible futures concept map, probable futures list, chart paper, and markers
	Initial Environmental Scan: Part 1	35–45 minutes	Copies of Task Sheet #7 (page 117), completed probable and preferred futures chart papers, copies of the Initial Environmental Scan Activity Sheet: Part 1 (Handout 2), blank paper, markers, and pens
	Initial Environmental Scan: Part 2	60–70 minutes	Probable and preferable futures lists, blank paper, pens, copies of the Initial Environmental Scan Activity Sheet: Part 2 (Handout 3), chart paper, and markers
Segment 4: What Are the Data and Questions for This Inquiry? (Chapter 5) *Approximately 7 hours*	Blocking the Canvas: Selecting Your Colors	140 minutes	Copies of Task Sheet #8 (page 118), results from the initial environmental scan, copies of Selecting Your Colors Activity Sheet (Handout 4), markers, chart paper, and pens

(Continued)

NOTE: Task Sheets are identified by page numbers in *Leading Schools in a Data-Rich World: Harnessing Data for School Improvement*. Handouts can be found within this guide, starting on page 42.

(Continued)

Segment	Activities	Time	Materials
Segment 4 (Continued)	Blocking the Canvas: From Indicator Categories to Questions	40 minutes	Copies of Blocking the Canvas: From Indicator Categories to Questions Activity Sheet (Handout 5), copies of the shared Selecting Your Colors Activity Sheet (Handout 4), pens, projector, computer, and screen (or chart paper and markers)
	Blocking the Canvas: From Questions to Data Sources	60–70 minutes	Copies of questions from Blocking the Canvas: From Indicator Categories to Questions Activity Sheet (Handout 5), Blocking the Canvas: From Questions to Data Sources Activity Sheet (Handout 6), pens, projector, screen, and a computer
	Blocking the Canvas: Data Quality	35 minutes	Copies of the Data Quality Activity Sheet (Handout 7) and pens
	Blocking the Canvas: What Is the Quality of Our Data?	110–120 minutes	Copies of Task Sheet #10 (pages 120–121), copies of the Questions About Data Quality Activity Sheet (Handout 8), data sources and quality information collected as a result of *Blocking the Canvas: From Questions to Data Sources* activity, and pens
Segment 5: How Do We Make Sense of the Data? (Chapters 5 and 6) *Approximately 7 hours*	First Strokes: Interpreting the Individual Data Sources	Data preparation, plus 60–90 minutes per data set	Prepared data, copies of Task Sheet #11 (page 122), pens, and copies of Interpreting the Individual Data Sources Activity Sheet (Handout 9)
	First Strokes: Constructing a Concept Map From Data Interpretations	90 minutes	Copies of completed Interpreting the Individual Data Sources Activity Sheet (Handout 9), copies of Task Sheet #11 (page 122), pens, chart paper, and markers
	The Image Grows: Consensus About Interpretations	210–240 minutes	Copies of Task Sheet #12 (page 123), copies of the concept map from the previous activity (*First Strokes: Constructing a Concept Map From Data Interpretations*), Consensus About Interpretations Activity Sheet (Handout 10), chart paper, markers, and sticky index cards
Segment 6: How Do We Do Something About What We Find? (Chapter 6) *Approximately 2 hours*	The Image Grows: Moving to Action	60 minutes	Copies of the Consensus About Interpretations Activity Sheet (Handout 10), skeleton action plan, pens, and copies of Task Sheet #13 (page 124)
	Displaying the Picture: Sharing the Learning	75 minutes	Copies of completed Task Sheet #13 (page 124), copies of completed Task Sheet #5 (page 115), and copies of Task Sheet #14 (page 125), chart paper, markers, and pens
Segment 7: Sustaining the Process (Chapter 7)	N/A	N/A	N/A

NOTE: Task Sheets are identified by page numbers in *Leading Schools in a Data-Rich World: Harnessing Data for School Improvement*. Handouts can be found within this guide, starting on page 42.

Overview of the Book

The book *Leading Schools in a Data-Rich World: Harnessing Data for School Improvement* was written for groups of people who are interested and committed to school improvement and who are willing to work together over time to use data in their school improvement process. School improvement is a never-ending process that involves routine attention to evidence-based decision making within the local context. In working through the concepts presented in the book, it is important for school leaders to secure the sincere engagement of the school faculty. Although engaging a whole school in thinking about data and how they can be used can be challenging, the benefits of collaborative inquiry are worth the effort.

Collaborative inquiry creates an opportunity for educators to search for and consider various sources of knowledge (both explicit and tacit) in order to investigate practices and ideas through a number of lenses, to put forward hypotheses, to challenge beliefs, and to pose more questions. When educators have an *inquiry habit of mind*, they have developed a *way of thinking* that is a dynamic iterative system for organizing ideas, seeking out information, and moving closer and closer to understanding some phenomenon. The work is intellectually challenging, collaborative, and intense. The reward for the hard work is becoming a culture of inquiry and having a mechanism to target improvement efforts. *Leading Schools in a Data-Rich World: Harnessing Data for School Improvement* and this accompanying *Facilitator's Guide* are support tools to help leaders create the conditions that are conducive to this kind of collaborative inquiry.

The book uses the metaphor of a painter painting a gallery full of images of a complex environment to provide a framework for the group to think about their work and the process of using data to learn about and communicate about their school with others, in the service of improvement. To successfully use the framework, the work must be embedded in ongoing school processes. It is important that people in the school do not perceive this work as an add-on—something else they have to do. They need to understand how using evidence to make decisions can be an integral and valuable part of their current work in supporting school priorities. This message must be communicated and endorsed by system leaders as you begin the process, and high-level encouragement must continue throughout the process.

Additional Resources for Facilitators

Corwin Press also offers a free 16-page resource titled *Tips for Facilitators* that includes practical strategies and tips for guiding a successful meeting. The information in this section describes different professional development opportunities, the principles of effective professional development, some characteristics of an effective facilitator, the responsibilities of the facilitator, and practical tips and strategies to make the meeting more successful. *Tips for Facilitators* is available for free download at the Corwin Press Web site (www.corwinpress.com, under "Other Resources").

We recommend that facilitators download a copy of *Tips for Facilitators* and review the characteristics and responsibilities of facilitators and professional development strategies for different types of work groups and settings.

Chapter-by-Chapter Study Guide

Facilitator's Guide to *Leading Schools in a Data-Rich World: Harnessing Data for School Improvement* by Lorna M. Earl and Steven Katz

Segment 1: What Do You Believe About Your School?

This segment is designed to engage the preconceptions of the participants. It is important to ascertain how the participants view and understand the school. Perceptions vary, and it is important to address which characteristics team members note, notice, and highlight as contextual descriptors of the local school context.

Chapter 1. Putting Data at the Center of School Improvement

Notes for Facilitators

- The use of data is a compelling driver in school improvement.

- A shift in public expectations has placed new demands on school leaders and teachers to relate data to their decisions in schools.

  - Historically, education professionals used their tacit knowledge and relied on their professional judgment to make the best decisions for schools. The public trusted this process.

○ Currently, education has become awash with data and accompanying accountability policies that have created public expectation that school leaders will use and respond to the data to improve student achievement. The public is looking for confirmation with external evidence.

- The shift in public expectations means that educators need to use data to improve schools in a systematic and deliberate way. Accountability policies insist that data be used, but may not take into account the new capacities that educators need in order to use data appropriately.

- Accountability that fosters a performance-oriented culture is at risk of undermining the tacit knowledge of educators. It is important to focus on building a learning-oriented culture that respects tacit and explicit knowledge and considers both together in decision making.

- Data can and should be used as a mechanism for having conversations about school processes, direction, results, capacity, and improvement.

- We are in an era of informed professionalism that regards accountability as a process for school improvement where educators are responsible for using data as part of a toolkit to understand current performance, formulate reasonable improvement plans, move into action, and monitor and assess the progress of schools.

- There are multiple uses for data. Understanding the purpose of the data prior to collecting them is important for making sense of them.

- Data become information, and information becomes knowledge when people make sense out of it through thoughtful conversations that shape the information to make it meaningful in their context. This gives them the foundation for wisdom—making wise decisions based on their new knowledge.

- The process is difficult, challenging, and requires a new set of thinking skills. It is important to support educators in their learning to develop a culture of inquiry in schools.

Discussion Questions

1. As a part of the education system, what is your experience with data in school decision making?
2. How do you feel about data?
3. What is (are) the purpose(s) for which data are collected and used in your school?

4. What is the relationship between data and accountability in your school?
5. How does your sense of professional responsibility relate to accountability in your school?
6. What kinds of learning opportunities would you benefit from?
7. What do you expect from this book (or workshop)?
8. How would you describe your school? How do you know?
9. How would others describe your school? How do you know?
10. What characteristics are important when describing a school?

Activities

● *Describe the Context of Your School*

Time: 45–50 minutes

Materials: Paper and pen

Give the participants 5 minutes to individually and silently reflect on how they see their school. Ask them to imagine that they are writing a letter to someone who will be visiting their school for the first time next month. This person has asked them for an honest description of what to expect.

Give the participants 10 minutes to individually and silently write their letter in note form. Insist that they be explicit about the characteristics of the school they believe are important school context descriptors.

Have the whole group form a circle. Explain that this activity is constructed to get a sense of what characteristics others in the group believe are important school context descriptors, to identify the similarities and differences between the perceptions of the individuals in the group, and to achieve a shared understanding of the school with the group. There are no right or wrong answers. At this point, listening is the most important activity for the participants in the group.

Give the group 10–15 minutes to share their notes. Ask individual participants to read their notes to the larger group and ask the rest of the group to listen silently. It is important that the group does not react but simply takes in the different perceptions of their school.

Give the group 15–20 minutes to share their insights on what they heard. Ask individual participants to share their thinking regarding how the group sees their school. This activity is not to reach a consensus on which characteristics are important in describing the school but to achieve an appreciation for the different perspectives. It is probable that there will be some differences in perception among group members. The dissimilarity can be used to foster discussions on the evidence individuals use to form opinions and judgments about the school.

Option. The facilitator can revisit these descriptions and redo this first task after preliminary data about the school have been collected and shared. If time permits, the facilitator can guide a discussion on the changes or lack of changes in the shared description of the school and the importance of good evidence to an informed opinion.

● *Beliefs About Accountability*

Time: 45 minutes

Materials: Copies of Task Sheet #2 (pages 111–112 of the book *Leading Schools in a Data-Rich World* by Lorna M. Earl and Steven Katz), chart paper, masking tape, and markers

This is an activity of *personal reflection* on individual and collective engagement with accountability measures in schools. It is important for participants to identify their beliefs about and their experiences with accountability in schools because explicating preconceptions is a fundamental prerequisite to new learning.

Give the participants 15 minutes to consider and answer the five questions on Task Sheet #2. Ask them to write their responses on a copy of the task sheet.

Give the participants 5 minutes to quietly read "Fear of Data and Evaluation" on page 4 of the book.

Post two pieces of chart paper on opposite walls. Write "Performance-Oriented Accountability" on one piece of chart paper and "Learning-Oriented Accountability" on the other.

Ask the participants to consider their answers to the five questions on Task Sheet #2 and stand next to the orientation they believe best represents their current situation. Give the groups 15 minutes to identify the characteristics of their current situation that made them move to a particular orientation. Identify a recorder in each of the two groups to write the key characteristics they identified on the corresponding chart paper.

Ask the groups to read the characteristics on each other's chart paper. Invite the participants to share their reflections on the similarities or differences between the two orientations.

● *Collective Beliefs About Accountability With Purpose*

Time: 30 minutes

Materials: Copies of Task Sheet #2 (pages 111–112 of the book *Leading Schools in a Data-Rich World* by Lorna M. Earl and Steven Katz), chart paper, masking tape, and markers

Give the participants 5 minutes to reread (or read) "Accountability Redefined" on pages 9–10 in the book. Ask the participants to individually complete the second question on the first page of Task Sheet #2: "What do you currently do to satisfy these requirements?" Encourage the individuals to really think about the desired state of their current accountability policies when answering the question.

Post a blank piece of chart paper on the third wall between the other two chart papers describing the characteristics of accountability orientations from the previous activity. Title the blank chart paper "Purpose of Use" and ask the participants to read the two sections on pages 12–15 in the book.

Lead a group reflection on how data can be used or has been used to move from a performance-oriented culture to a learning-oriented culture. Write down the key ideas that emerge from the group on the chart paper. (This can be done on a computer using a word processing program. It is important that the facilitator capture the ideas from the group so that they can be revisited later in the process.)

Segment 2: Capacities for Using Data for Decision Making

This segment is about understanding the capacities for engaging in the process of using data for decision making. Developing a culture of inquiry in a school requires support for new ways of thinking, or an inquiry habit of mind. People in the school will have different levels of knowledge, skills, and experience in this area. It is important to identify the experts and novices to appropriately build capacities as you move through the process.

Chapter 2. Using Data for Informed Decision Making

Notes for Facilitators

- Internal accountability that is founded on using data for improvement-focused conversations places school decisions in the hands of educators and requires that they habitually use data to rethink and reconstruct their professional knowledge and practice. This demand for informed professionalism requires educators to develop an inquiry habit of mind, become data literate, and create a culture of inquiry in their school community.

- A learning organization has a culture of inquiry when the whole school community continually engages in an iterative process where they question what is happening in their school and they seek evidence to collectively understand the situation. People with an inquiry habit of mind actively seek out information that will help them rethink their practice and focus their questions.

- An inquiry habit of mind depends on data literacy. A data-literate leader guides the school in using data appropriately in a culture of inquiry. Data-literate leaders:

  o Recognize that data should be used with a purpose in mind. Purpose is determined by the needs of the school.

  o Recognize that data are representations of ideas that contain some degree of uncertainty, and are knowledgeable enough to appropriately identify sound and unsound data and how to use them for reasonable decisions.

  o Are familiar with the principles of measurement that are used to generate data and understand the conventions used in measurement so that they know what degree of certainty they can have in their data when they make their decisions.

  o Are familiar with the different kinds of data (e.g., qualitative and quantitative) that they can use to support the inquiry process.

  o Value the interpretation of data through a commitment to thinking about the data and moving them from being representations of ideas to information through a thoughtful, systematic process of considering multiple possibilities without preconceived judgment. Information moves from being interpretations to knowledge through the social process of collaborative inquiry.

  o Know and respect the audience(s). Leaders should present the data, interpretations, and key messages from the inquiry with due consideration for the needs and interests of their different audiences.

- In a school with a culture of inquiry, the school routinely uses data to make sense of the environment and to think about the future. School leaders need to foster a culture of inquiry to be able to use data to make decisions. To create a culture of inquiry, a school leader:

  o Creates the conditions for others to engage with the data in a process that promotes insights and makes tacit knowledge explicit for others.

  o Uses data to create a sense of urgency that motivates educators to engage in the challenging work of identifying the current situation of their school and, subsequently, deciding on the direction of their school.

  o Makes time for educators to make sense of the data through a collective process where they can think, argue, reflect, share, and thoughtfully respond to the information in a meaningful way for school improvement.

o Invites "critical friends" with expertise in using data for decision making to support the school. A critical friend offers open, honest, and gentle critique of the situation and process.

Discussion Questions

1. What kinds of discussions about data currently occur in your school? (Think about how, where, when, and among whom data are discussed throughout the year.)
2. How do people in your school feel about data?
3. How do people use data in your school?
4. What is the level of data literacy across the different stakeholders in your school? Who has relevant expertise in your school, district, or community?
5. How could your school benefit from fostering a culture of inquiry?
6. What actions could you take to enhance a culture of inquiry in your school?

Activities

● *Self-Assessment of Capacities for Leading in a Data-Rich World*

Time: 10–15 minutes

Materials: Copies of Task Sheet #3 (page 113 of the book *Leading Schools in a Data-Rich World* by Lorna M. Earl and Steven Katz)

This activity is a *personal reflection* of each participant's key capacities for leading in a data-rich world.

Give the participants 10–15 minutes to individually complete a copy of Task Sheet #3. Tell them to use the descriptions of the key capacities for informed professionalism on pages 18–22 in the book. As they complete the self-assessment, invite the participants to write any questions they have about any of the capacities. The completed task sheet should be put aside for later use when the participants write their journal entry for this segment.

● *Capacities for Leading in a Data-Rich World*

Time: 90 minutes

Materials: Copies of Task Sheet #3 (page 113 of the book *Leading Schools in a Data-Rich World* by Lorna M. Earl and Steven Katz), notepads, and pens

This *panel and reaction panel* activity promotes a common understanding of the capacities for an inquiry habit of mind among the participants. The facilitator needs to be familiar with the key capacities to support the dialogue and foster a common understanding in the group.

Divide the participants into groups of four to six people. Identify a "panel group" and a "reaction panel" for each of the three areas introduced in Chapter 2: (1) "An Inquiry Habit of Mind," (2) "Data Literacy," and (3) "A Culture of Inquiry." (If there are more than three groups, divide the capacities within an area and assign them to panel groups. For example, have one group be responsible for the panel discussion of the first three capacities of being Data Literate and the other group be responsible for the last three listed capacities that describe being Data Literate.)

Give each panel group 15–20 minutes to prepare a 10-minute presentation about their views of the capacities listed in Task Sheet #3 for their group's area of focus (e.g., Data Literacy). The presentation should include their description of the capacities and illustrative examples of the capacities from their experiences. The panel should use real-life examples to discuss how each capacity can be recognized in practice.

At the end of each presentation, give the complementary reaction panel 10 minutes to react to the presentation of the panel group with a focus on clarifying key features of the capacities and how to recognize them in practice.

● Building a Culture of Inquiry in the School Community

Time: 30 minutes

Materials: Chart paper

This *debate* activity draws out the conflicting views of participants to articulate the arguments leaders face when trying to support capacity building for creating a culture of inquiry in the school community.

Divide the room into two halves and assign one side as the "pros" and the other side as the "cons." Post pieces of chart paper at opposite sides of the room. As a visual reminder for each group, write the PRO or CON activity questions and the four key capacities for a culture of inquiry (as shown on page 15 of this guide) on each chart paper, respectively.

Give each group 10–15 minutes to prepare the key points that address the PRO or CON questions for each of the four capacities. Identify a recorder in each group and ask them to write down the key points on the chart paper.

Facilitate a debate between the two groups. Encourage the participants to articulate their points and constructively respond to the points of the opposing group. The purpose of the activity is to identify potential challenges and benefits to building a culture of inquiry in schools.

PRO		CON	
What are some actions school leaders can take to support a culture of inquiry in the school community?		What resistance can school leaders expect when trying to support building a culture of inquiry in the school community?	
Involve others in interpreting and engaging with the data		Involve others in interpreting and engaging with the data	
Stimulate an internal sense of urgency		Stimulate an internal sense of urgency	
Make time		Make time	
Use "critical friends"		Use "critical friends"	

Journal Writing

Revisit your completed Task Sheet #3 self-assessment. Pick two capacities that you would like to focus on improving and answer the following questions:

1. To what extent did your understanding of your chosen capacities change? How?

2. What can you do to build your capacity in those two areas in the next year?

Chapter 3. Cultivating the Qualities of Data-Driven Leadership

Notes for Facilitators

- Making evidence-informed decisions is a continuous process that is iterative, nonlinear, and requires educators to rethink the current situation and direction of the school on a regular basis.

- The process of using data to portray a school is like the process of painting a picture of a garden. Artists first think about the garden and carefully plan how to best portray it, changing their approaches as they discover more about the garden.

- It is common for educators to attend to whatever data are readily available (e.g., test scores) and jump to conclusions about what the data mean. A data-literate leader first thinks and plans an inquiry approach, and then leads the school community through an appropriate process to consider the data that are relevant and helps them think as they go through the decision-making process.

- There are six connected steps to painting a data picture of a school. Each step is part of building capacity for informed professionalism in schools (see page 25 of the book *Leading Schools in a Data-Rich World* by Lorna M. Earl and Steven Katz).

  o Having an *inquiry habit of mind* means reflecting on the current state of the school, the direction of the school, and the process by which to achieve certain goals. (1) *Setting the canvas* and (2) *planning the picture* clarify the priority issues, key participants, preferred direction, and current state of understanding surrounding the issues.

  o *Data literacy* is required to appreciate the formal and informal data that can serve as tools to paint the picture. (3) *Blocking the canvas* and (4) *the first strokes* are about setting parameters on what data will be used for this picture

and making some tentative first steps to appreciate the quality of the data and what they can appropriately portray.
- o *Building a culture of inquiry* relies on collaborative professional learning to create and share knowledge. (5) *The image grows* and (6) *displaying the picture* correspond to the various interpretations that arise from professional discussions about the data and sharing them with multiple audiences to stimulate action and decide on next steps.

- When a picture is completed, new questions arise and other issues need to be addressed. For learning organizations that are committed to continuous improvement, the process never stops. The school should be working toward a gallery of paintings.

Discussion Questions

1. What steps to painting a data-rich picture do I already take in my school? How would someone else observe this engagement?
2. What are the capacities I will need to cultivate as a leader in a data-rich school?
3. How will I cultivate key capacities during the process of painting a data-driven picture in my school?

Activities

● *Painting a Data-Rich Picture*

Time: 20–30 minutes

Materials: Copies of the Metaphor Reflection Activity Sheet (Handout 1) and pens

This is a *paired sharing metaphor reflection* exercise to help participants understand the metaphor of painting a data-rich picture in their school.

Facilitate a large-group discussion about how educators engage, formally and informally, in the painting steps in their school. Emphasize the areas of familiarity some participants will have with some of the steps in the process. Invite participants to offer examples from their experiences with school improvement processes, and help them relate those experiences to the steps in the painting metaphor.

Hand out a copy of the Metaphor Reflection Activity Sheet (Handout 1) to each participant. Given them 5 minutes to:

- Mark the column where they currently invest most of their effort.
- Mark the column that they need to work on most to engage the school community. In that column, ask them to note why they think this is an important place to invest more effort.

Give the participants 10 minutes to share their completed Metaphor Reflection Activity Sheets with a partner (in pairs).

Journal Writing

What are the steps in painting a data-rich picture with which you are least familiar? How will you access resources to build your capacity to lead this step in your school?

Segment 3: What Is the Context and Direction of This Inquiry?

This segment is about establishing the priorities and people for school improvement. This segment walks you through the preparatory steps to focus school efforts. The polymorphic nature of schools means that it is easy to move in many directions at the same time, leaving the impression of a scattered process. These preparatory steps offer a process by which people in the school can identify a common priority or vision toward which they can work together.

Chapter 4. Developing an Inquiry Habit of Mind

Notes for Facilitators

- Setting the canvas and planning the picture are part of the process to develop an inquiry habit of mind. These are the preparatory steps to painting a data-rich picture. These steps are important in keeping the process manageable, inclusive, relevant, and successful.

- *Setting the canvas* is the first stage of the process. Schools are complex organizations that always have a number of issues that need attention for school improvement according to different stakeholders. Setting the canvas prioritizes the key issues, makes the roles of teacher leaders and the school community explicit, and identifies the audiences.

- Once the priority is identified, it is important to find out what is known about the issue and in which direction to lead the school. *Planning this picture* is a way for leaders to develop the strategy that will help them carry the vision into reality.

- Moving from vague images of areas of concern to detailed descriptions of intentions and what those intentions look like in terms of school practices and outcomes is at the core of moving toward a preferred future.

Discussion Questions

1. Why do you want the data? How do you expect the data to fit your purpose(s)?
2. Given these different purposes, what are the different roles for each stakeholder?
3. Who is already involved and who should be included in the process? How can those who need to be involved be included?
4. What is your vision for your school? To what extent is this vision a shared one? How do you know?

Activities

● *Purpose, Context, and Roles*

Time: 30–40 minutes

Materials: Copies of Task Sheet #4 (page 114 of the book *Leading Schools in a Data-Rich World* by Lorna M. Earl and Steven Katz), index cards, scissors, and pens

Refer to Assignment #4 (page 33), "Purpose, Context, and Roles."

Prior to the session, ask the participants to individually complete the chart on Task Sheet #4. Ask them to identify the most pressing and compelling issue and the rationale for their choice. If possible, before the session, collect the completed charts and cut up the rows so that one issue and its accompanying rationale are on one piece of paper. Otherwise, collect the papers at the session.

Post all of the pieces of paper with the issues and rationale on a wall in a random order. Invite each participant to quickly present the priority or priorities they identified as being important and the rationale for their choice.

At the end of the presentations, ask the participants to write out on blank index cards the three issues they believe to be the top priorities. On the adjacent wall in the room, post three pieces of chart paper titled "Priorities." Invite the participants to place their three cards on the chart paper. Give the teams 20 minutes to work through the grouping of the issues. During this activity, the facilitator needs to engage with the group to make sure that all voices are heard.

When the priority groupings are complete, conduct a *quiet meeting*. Give the participants 5 minutes to sit quietly and reflect on the issues that have the most index cards. Invite the participants to share their individual ideas about the priorities they see on the wall, and remind the participants that they should not offer any reactions to the comments being shared. The power of this approach is in the listening process.

Select the three issues that were identified by the team as the most urgent and important to investigate. These will be the three issues with the most "votes" on the wall.

● *Identifying Audiences*

Time: 30–40 minutes

Materials: Copies of Task Sheet #5 (page 115 of the book *Leading Schools in a Data-Rich World* by Lorna M. Earl and Steven Katz), markers, pens, two different colors of sticky notes, chart paper, and masking tape

Post a piece of chart paper on the wall and title it "Potential Audiences." Conduct a *round robin* exercise with the group. The facilitator or a recorder needs to be ready to write the ideas on the posted chart paper. Starting with one side of the room, ask the participants to name *one* potential stakeholder that is, or could be, involved or affected by the planning process. The recorder writes down whatever is said, verbatim. Each participant is invited to offer only one idea that has not already been listed on the chart paper. When everyone has had one opportunity to offer a suggestion, initiate a second round and tell the participants that they can "pass" their turn if their selected audience member has already been identified by another participant and is listed at the front of the room.

The chart paper with the round robin results will offer a complete list of the potential audiences. This list will be used for the rest of this activity.

Refer to Assignment #5 on page 35 in the book addressing "Identifying Audiences."

Post the chart papers on separate walls in the room and title each one with one of the priority issues identified at the end of Assignment #4. Divide the participants into three groups and identify one of the priority issues for each group to work on during this activity. Ask the groups to move to the appropriate chart paper posted in the room.

Allow the participants 10 minutes to identify the audiences that would be affected by the priority they are addressing in their group. Ask each group to write the names and positions of all the people currently involved in the planning of their group's identified issue on one color of sticky notes. Then ask them to write the names and positions of the people who should be involved but are not currently involved on the second color sticky notes. Have the group members place notes with the names on the chart paper. Ask them to use the marker to draw arrows linking people together in their working relationships given their roles and responsibilities in the school or district.

Bring the three groups back together into the larger group. Post the chart papers from each group on the front wall next to one another and next to the list of audiences from the round robin. Give the whole group 5 minutes to sit quietly and note the similarities and differences between the audiences identified for each issue. Guide a group discussion to consider the audiences for the three issues. Finally, have the group consider whether all the relevant stakeholders identified in the round robin were included in the audiences identified in the smaller groups.

● *Possible Futures*

Time: 80–90 minutes

Materials: Copies of Task Sheet #6 (page 116 of the book *Leading Schools in a Data-Rich World* by Lorna M. Earl and Steven Katz), chart paper, markers, masking tape, and sticky notes

Give the participants 5 minutes to read "Possible Futures" on pages 37–38 in the book.

Lead a brief (5-minute) discussion on what could be included in the possible future of the school. Encourage the participants to use their imagination.

Write the three priority issues on a single chart paper posted at the front of the room. Invite the participants to articulate the factors that are likely to be important to the school for the priority issues (e.g., student achievement, student attitudes, teacher turnover, parent involvement, teaching assessments, instructional practice, student demographics, community development) and write them down on the posted chart paper.

Give the participants 5–10 minutes to write down those factors that are likely or unlikely to change in their context on sticky notes.

Organize the participants into groups of five or six and give each group a piece of chart paper with a priority issue marked at the top. Give the groups 20 minutes to post the factors they wrote on the sticky notes on the chart paper. Ask them to link the factors in a reasonable organization that shows how they are related. They can use markers to help clarify the relationships between the factors.

When they complete the organization task, ask each participant to think of two other stakeholders with whom they work who are not in the session (e.g., parents, students, teachers, administrators, administrative assistant, or nurse) and guess what kind of ideas those people might offer if they were present. Give the group another 10 minutes to add the "new" ideas to their chart papers and reposition any of the sticky notes as necessary.

Ask the groups to place their chart papers next to one another at the front. Ask the participants to silently reflect on the similarities and differences that exist between the possible futures. Guide a whole-group discussion on the possible futures of the school. Move the sticky notes, reorganize them, and draw connecting lines to build a concept map that represents the results of the whole-group discussion as the ideas emerge.

Facilitator's Guide to *Leading Schools in a Data-Rich World*

● *Probable Futures*

Time: 30–40 minutes

Materials: Copies of Task Sheet #6 (page 116 of the book *Leading Schools in a Data-Rich World* by Lorna M. Earl and Steven Katz), the possible futures concept map that was completed in the previous activity, chart paper, blank paper, pens, and markers

Post the possible futures concept map at the front of the room. If there was a pause (one day or more) between the *Possible Futures* activity and this one, take 5 minutes to revisit the concept map with the whole group.

Give the group 5 minutes to read "Probable Futures" on pages 38–39 in the book.

Give the participants 10 minutes to describe what they think their school is like at present in as much detail as possible. Ask the participants to use the same categories as posted in the concept map and Task Sheet #6. Require the participants to provide the evidence for their beliefs (i.e., how do they form their opinions about their school?).

Organize the participants into pairs. Give the pairs 10 minutes to predict what will most likely occur in the next couple of years if nothing changes in their school. Ask them to use the factors identified in the possible futures concept map and record their list of ideas on a piece of paper.

Organize the pairs into groups of four where each pair shares their joint probable future predictions with the other pair. Give them 10 minutes to record their combined thinking onto a piece of paper. Continue to recombine the groups (i.e., two groups of four joined to make one group of eight) until the whole group is brought back together.

When the whole group is combined, lead the whole group in writing out the list of factors for the probable future of the school on a piece of chart paper posted on the front wall.

● *Preferable Futures*

Time: 35–45 minutes

Materials: Copies of Task Sheet #6 (page 116 of the book *Leading Schools in a Data-Rich World* by Lorna M. Earl and Steven Katz), possible futures concept map, probable futures list, chart paper, and markers

Post the possible futures map and preferable futures list on the front wall adjacent to each other. Post a blank piece of chart paper titled "Preferred Futures" next to the other two chart papers.

Give the participants 10 minutes to individually record their detailed descriptions of their preferred future when answering the last question on Task Sheet #6: "Where would we like to go? Create a detailed scenario that describes the future as you prefer it to be."

Ask the participants to include the factors identified as important in the *Possible Futures* activity in their response.

Lead a *fishbowl* sharing discussion. Ask three or four participants to form a discussion circle to come to a common description of the preferred future. Have the rest of the participants form a listening circle around the inner sharing circle. Invite two to four new participants into the inner circle to continue the discussion every 7–10 minutes. Continue inviting more members from the listening circle into the inner circle until the whole group is included.

When the whole group forms the inner circle, the facilitator should recapitulate the main points of what the preferred future of the school looks like and record the ideas on the preferred futures chart paper at the front of the room.

● *Initial Environmental Scan*

This activity is conducted over two workshop sessions. Part 1 of the activity gives participants a scaffold for collecting information that represents the current state of the school for the priority issues. Part 2 of the activity gives the participants the opportunity to make sense of the information that they collected and revisit the priorities given the new information.

Initial Environmental Scan: Part 1

Time: 35–45 minutes

Materials: Copies of Task Sheet #7 (page 117 of the book *Leading Schools in a Data-Rich World* by Lorna M. Earl and Steven Katz), completed probable and preferred futures chart papers, copies of the Initial Environmental Scan Activity Sheet: Part 1 (Handout 2), blank paper, markers, and pens

Post the probable and preferable futures chart papers completed in the previous session on the front wall. Write the three priority issues on separate pieces of blank paper with a marker. Place those papers marked with priorities on three separate tables in three corners of the room.

Invite the participants to walk to the issue that interests them most, personally and/or professionally.

In their small groups, have the participants elect a "group lead." This person will be responsible for recording the outcome of this activity, coordinating the group effort after the session, collecting the information from the group, and reporting back to the larger group in Part 2 of this initial environmental scan activity. Give the participants a copy of the Initial Environmental Scan Activity Sheet: Part 1 (Handout 2).

Give the groups 25 minutes to discuss and decide the important factors on which they will focus. Encourage the groups to use the probable and preferred futures chart papers at the front wall to identify key factors. Ask them to identify what they think they already know about the factor, what data inform their perceptions, and what they could do to find out more about the issue? At the end of the activity, each group should have a game plan for how to collect more information on the issue.

Ask the participants to come back together into a single group. Give each group lead 3–5 minutes to briefly present the environmental scan strategy they developed in their group to the whole group.

Tell the groups they are now responsible for following through with their environmental scan strategy before the next session. Ask each group to prepare a presentation activity. The presentations should answer the following:

- What did the group learn from locating or collecting the additional data?
- To what extent does the information gathered resonate with the probable future described by the group?

Initial Environmental Scan: Part 2

Time: 60–70 minutes

Materials: Probable and preferable futures lists, blank paper, pens, copies of the Initial Environmental Scan Activity Sheet: Part 2 (Handout 3), chart paper, and markers

Post the probable and preferable futures chart papers completed in the previous session on the front wall. Invite each group to offer a 10–15 minute presentation on their priority area. At the end of each presentation, invite the other two groups to ask questions and make comments regarding how the new information interacts with the probable future described in the previous session (posted on the front wall). If the information changes the probable future, then a new probable future chart needs to be created in a whole-group discussion.

Coordinate a *jigsaw* exercise. Organize the participants into groups of three by selecting one person from each of the three priority groups to form the new groups. Ask the groups of three to consider the gap between the probable and preferred futures using the Initial Environmental Scan Activity Sheet: Part 2 (Handout 3). Give them 20 minutes to complete the sheet and decide on the most urgent area. Recombine the groups of three into groups of six. Give them 10 minutes to combine their thinking onto a single record sheet. Continue to recombine the groups (i.e., two groups of six joined to make one group of twelve) until the whole group is brought back together and one urgent priority is identified.

The facilitator leads the final group. Ask the participants to review the possible "finalists" for the urgent priorities. List them at the front of the room. Invite the group to consider the final priorities and suggest criteria that could help the group decide which one to select (e.g., is the priority something that the school has any control over? If the priority is, does the priority involve the whole school?). Lead a discussion on how each priority satisfies the group criteria to identify the one that is most important for the group to pursue.

Given the extent of the gaps identified (last column), what is the most urgent priority area? What is your rationale for this choice?

Segment 4: What Are the Data and Questions for This Inquiry?

This segment is about moving on the common priority. Often, a lack of data is not necessarily the problem. It is how to choose, manage, and understand the data so that they can be effectively used to help educators make decisions rather than overwhelm them. There needs to be an alignment between the priority, the indicators, the questions, and the data. When these pieces are appropriately linked, it is possible to make sense of the data. This segment offers a framework for aligning those pieces.

Chapter 5. Becoming Data Literate

Notes for Facilitators

- *Blocking the canvas* and *first strokes* describe a thinking process that addresses issues in a systematic and iterative way to explore a priority.

- Often, educators jump to action without sufficient attention to identifying the problem. *Blocking the canvas* engages the school in systematically exploring priority issues to identify the pertinent questions and to construct a sketch of the data they will require to address the questions or to help pose more focused questions.

- When the data are collected, they need to be analyzed and interpreted for meaning. *First strokes* is a mechanism by which leaders can support educators in using their knowledge of the school to make sense of the data. This stage involves both individual and collective interpretation.

- The process of moving from describing intentions to constructing a data-picture requires strong leadership. School leaders need to offer encouragement, structure, and direction to motivate a collective effort for the people involved to participate in a complex and time-consuming process. At the same time, school leaders need to motivate the participants to explore ideas and different interpretations, reflect on their knowledge, and allow for the inherent ambiguity of this iterative process.

Discussion Questions

1. What do you think you know about the priority? How sure are you about what you know? How open are you to being wrong?
2. What kinds of questions would help you challenge or confirm what you think you know?
3. What are the important questions that need to be answered about the priority?
4. What kinds of data would help you consider questions about your priority?
5. To what extent are the data you need accessible? What kinds of steps can you take to acquire the data you need?
6. To what extent are the data you have trustworthy? How do you know?
7. What data could you collect to help answer the important questions? How do you think these data would be useful?

Activities

NOTE: A critical friend can be very useful in the Blocking the Canvas and First Strokes activities. The purpose and role of a critical friend is introduced on page 21 of the book *Leading Schools in a Data-Rich World* by Lorna M. Earl and Steven Katz.

●   *Blocking the Canvas: Selecting Your Colors*

Time: 140 minutes

Materials: Copies of Task Sheet #8 (page 118 of the book *Leading Schools in a Data-Rich World* by Lorna M. Earl and Steven Katz), results from the initial environmental scan, copies of Selecting Your Colors Activity Sheet (Handout 4), markers, chart paper, and pens

Ask the participants to review their completed Initial Environmental Scan Activity Sheet: Part 2 (Handout 3). Give them 5 minutes to read over their answer to the last question, that focused the group on the most important priority: *What is the most urgent priority area? What is your rationale for this choice?*

Give the group 10 minutes to individually read "What Indicator Categories?" on pages 49–51 in the book.

Lead a whole-group discussion addressing each of the indicator categories listed in the book section. Ask the participants to give examples of data that would fit into each category. Encourage them to think of one example of data they already have and one that they could collect. It is important that the whole group feels comfortable with the definitions of these indicator categories. Most groups will have participants with a range of knowledge about indicators and data. The facilitator needs to simultaneously draw on the expertise of the participants in the group and draw out questions from the neophytes in the group. A heterogeneous group is an asset for fostering clarifications for a well-articulated and illustrated common understanding of indicator categories.

Place the participants into groups of three or four participants. Each group needs a strong facilitator who will ensure that the individuals all participate and stay on task because this is a challenging task that requires sustained concentration, reflection, and listening. Give a copy of Selecting Your Colors Activity Sheet (Handout 4) to each person.

Give the groups 40 minutes to complete the second column of the activity sheet by answering the question "What do you already know about each indicator category in relation to your priority?" Ask the participants to use both the existing data and their tacit knowledge to answer the question.

Post blank chart paper on the wall next to each group and place markers next to each sheet of chart paper. Randomly assign two indicator categories to each group. Ask each group to title the chart papers with their assigned indicator category so that there is only one category per chart paper. Give the participants 10 minutes to record what their group knows about each of their assigned indicator categories (the second column in the activity sheet), identifying what they know from existing data in one marker color and using another marker color for their tacit knowledge.

Assign a color to each group. Ask the groups to move clockwise to the next group's set of chart papers. Give the group 10–12 minutes to:

1. Read the information on the chart paper on what is known about the priority area.
2. Determine to what extent the information written on the chart paper is different from what their group identified as being known about each indicator category during the 40-minute group exercise.

   a. If there is no difference, ask them to use their group's color to mark a check on the chart paper and move to the next indicator category.
   b. If there is additional information, ask the group to discuss the extent of the difference and how it changes how the priority area is understood. They should use their group's color to write the additional information about the priority area on the chart paper.
   c. If there is information the group believes is incorrect or questionable, ask the group to discuss the inconsistency and, using

their group color, write down the information they have that challenges the idea on the chart paper.

3. Move clockwise to the next group's set of chart papers.

Invite everyone back to a whole-group discussion. Walk to each of the indicator categories (chart papers) and ask any group who made a change to the chart paper justify their decision to add or change the information. Welcome any disagreements at this point and push the group to discuss and describe what additional information they would need to settle the inconsistency in "knowledge" about the priority area.

Ask the participants to return to their groups. Give them 30–40 minutes to complete the third column on their activity sheet given their shared understanding of what they know about the priority in each indicator category. Ask them to consider what other information they might want to better examine the priority. Identify a recorder to mark the additional information on the corresponding chart paper.

Ask the small groups to report back to the whole group on the two indicator categories they were originally assigned. As each group reports back to the whole group, invite the other participants to comment on the extent to which the additional information matches what they identified in their group.

Once the activity is completed, identify someone to take all of the chart papers and enter the group answers into an electronic copy of the table. Have them send a copy of the shared Selecting Your Colors Activity Sheet to all the participants within a week of the session.

- *Blocking the Canvas: From Indicator Categories to Questions*

Time: 40 minutes

Materials: Copies of Blocking the Canvas: From Indicator Categories to Questions Activity Sheet (Handout 5), copies of the shared Selecting Your Colors Activity Sheet (Handout 4), pens, projector, computer, and screen (or chart paper and markers)

Prior to the session, prepare the activity sheets by building on the electronic copy of the completed Selecting Your Colors Activity Sheet (Handout 4) from the previous activity. Replace the last column ("Additional Information") with a new blank column titled "Questions." The activity sheet will have writing in the first two columns and nothing in the third column.

Distribute the activity sheet to all the participants. Select an indicator category that does not have a lot of current information identified in the second column. Use that indicator to conduct a *think- out-loud demonstration* of how to "translate" the current information into questions. Ask two participants to join you in constructing the questions. Start by explaining to the group that you are going to demonstrate the kind of conversation they will need to have to construct the questions. As you engage in the think-out-loud demonstration, make sure that you model the work of this activity by:

1. Including the participation of the two volunteer participants.
2. Discussing the thinking process of changing the current information into questions while being sensitive to the fact that some participants may believe the current information is established knowledge.
3. Asking if the questions developed are specific enough, or if the language allows for multiple interpretations.
4. Asking if the questions developed are biased. Do they facilitate exploring sources of data that could either confirm or challenge what we think we know about our priority?
5. Asking if the questions being asked can be considered by appealing to data.

At the front of the room, project onto a screen (or write on a chart paper) the following three questions:

1. Are the questions we developed specific enough? Does the language we used allow for multiple interpretations?
2. Are the questions leading to one kind of answer? Do the questions facilitate exploring sources of data that could either confirm or challenge what we think we know?
3. Are the questions ones that can be considered by appealing to data?

Instruct the small groups to consider the questions at the front of the room when completing this activity. Organize the participants into groups of two or three and assign two indicator categories to each group. It may be prudent to assign only one indicator category to the group that is assigned student achievement. Give the participants 20 minutes to deliberate on the ideas in the indicator category that were generated in the last session and turn the ideas into questions that might be considered by appealing to data. Ask each indicator group to record their questions on their activity sheets.

When the participants have completed constructing their questions, draw their attention to the "Additional Information" column in the table on the shared Selecting Your Colors Activity Sheet. Give the group 10–15 minutes to deliberate on the extent to which the "Additional Information" changes any of the questions they developed. Invite them to change any of the questions, and/or add questions to their Blocking the Canvas: From Indicator Categories to Questions Activity Sheets (Handout 5).

Journal Writing

Think of someone in your school who often has a different opinion from yours regarding the current state of the school. Think of the questions you developed in *Blocking the Canvas: From Indicator Categories to Questions* and forecast how data will help to shed light on the situation for both you and your colleague.

How would you approach your colleague with the question(s) and the pertinent data to invite a constructive discussion?

● *Blocking the Canvas: From Questions to Data Sources*

Time: 60–70 minutes

Materials: Copies of questions from Blocking the Canvas: From Indicator Categories to Questions Activity Sheet (Handout 5), Blocking the Canvas: From Questions to Data Sources Activity Sheet (Handout 6), pens, projector, screen, and a computer

Continue the *think-out-loud demonstration* using the indicator category selected for the demonstration in the previous activity (*Blocking the Canvas: From Indicator Categories to Questions*). Project the questions previously developed on the wall so the whole group can see them. Give the participants 5 minutes to use the information on pages 53–54 in the book as a reference to individually and silently think about the evidence that would help them consider the questions projected at the front of the room.

Ask two participants to join you to identify the data sources that would help address the questions. Project a copy of the Blocking the Canvas: From Indicator Categories to Questions Activity Sheet (Handout 5). Key in the data sources you identify with the two volunteers so that you complete the table on the activity sheet during the demonstration. As you engage in the think-out-loud demonstration, make sure that you model the work of this activity by:

1. Including the participation of the two volunteers.
2. Discussing the thinking process when identifying useful evidence.
3. Asking if the data source would also fit into another indicator category.
4. Asking where the data could be located.
5. Discussing the most efficient and effective procedure to access the data. Include details such as: Who is the best person to locate the data, how that person can access the data, and what is a reasonable timeline?

At the front of the room, project onto a screen (or write on a chart paper) the following questions:

1. Does the data source fit into another category?
2. Where can the data be located?
3. Who will access the data? How will this person access the data? When can we reasonably expect the data?

Tell the indicator groups to consider these questions when completing this activity. Organize the participants into the same groups of two or three as in the previous activity (*Blocking the Canvas: From Indicator Categories to Questions*). Tell each group that they are responsible for the same indicator category as in the previous activity. Give the participants 30 minutes to complete the Blocking the Canvas: From Questions to Data Sources Activity Sheet (Handout 6) considering the questions projected up front. Have the group record their ideas on their activity sheets.

Give the whole group 10–15 minutes to communicate with one another regarding the next steps (last column in the activity sheet). It is important to get a commitment from the named participants to locate the data sources for the next session. Identify a responsible individual to collect the completed activity sheets from the groups, create a single electronic file of the information on the activity sheets, and distribute the document to all the participants within the next 2 days.

● *Blocking the Canvas: Data Quality*

Time: 35 minutes

Materials: Copies of the Data Quality Activity Sheet (Handout 7) and pens

Lead a *read and discuss* exercise of the three characteristics of data quality described in the book: Reliability, validity, and reference points. Give the participants 10 minutes to individually and silently read pages 57–58 of the book *Leading Schools in a Data-Rich World* by Lorna M. Earl and Steven Katz. Ask the participants to jot down reflective notes on the descriptions they read on reliability, validity, and reference points.

Lead a whole-group discussion to arrive at a common understanding of all three terms. Invite the participants to share their comments and describe each of the terms in their own words. Ask the participants to come up with examples from their own work where they consider reliability, validity, and reference points.

Distribute copies of the Data Quality Activity Sheet (Handout 7) and give the participants 5 minutes to write down some notes that will remind them of the common definition of each term. Lead a whole-group brainstorming session on where the information on reliability, validity, and reference points can be located when accessing data sources. Ask the participants to take notes on their activity sheets and remind them that this sheet will serve as a reference tool during the next activity when they access data sources.

This completed activity sheet should be helpful in accessing information on reliability, validity, and reference points when you access data sources to block the canvas.

● *Blocking the Canvas: What Is the Quality of Our Data?*

Time: 110–120 minutes

Materials: Copies of Task Sheet #10 (pages 120–121 of the book *Leading Schools in a Data-Rich World* by Lorna M. Earl and Steven Katz), copies of the Questions About Data Quality Activity Sheet (Handout 8), data sources and quality information collected as a result of the *Blocking the Canvas: From Questions to Data Sources* activity, and pens

Facilitators will need to be diligent to keep the participants on task and encourage them throughout this activity. This is a section that can be difficult and uncomfortable for many educators. Educators can become disengaged because of a lack of interest in the finer details of data, or become cynical regarding the use of data because all data contain a degree of error. It is important to invite a conversation that will balance the skepticism with realism so that data-based decision making can become evidence-informed decision making.

The participants should have read pages 58–63 of the book *Leading Schools in a Data-Rich World* by Lorna M. Earl and Steven Katz prior to the meeting. Conduct a 10- to 15-minute *quiet meeting*. Invite the participants to individually share their reflections on the example in the text on pages 58–63. No reaction is given to these comments. Facilitators should absorb the participants' reflections to gauge how much encouragement and differential support will be required for the participants during this activity.

Place a copy of Questions About Data Quality Activity Sheet (Handout 8) on each of the tables where a small group will be working.

Invite the participants who were responsible for accessing the data sources from the demonstration indicator category to join you for another *demonstration* exercise.

Remind the group of the questions and data sources identified in the think-out-loud demonstrations from the previous activities in *Blocking the Canvas*. Conduct a think-out-loud demonstration of the data quality activity. As you model the activity, make sure that you and the volunteers articulate your thinking for the benefit of the whole group.

Ask the participant responsible for accessing the data to lead the exercise in each group. Ask the lead to use the questions about data quality to help guide the discussion. The lead will present the information that she or he collected to the small group. The group will look through the documentation together to answer all the questions about each data source.

Ask the participants to get into their indicator groups. Give the groups 60 minutes to work through their data sources. When the quality of a data source is established and the group decides how much attention it deserves, the lead should rotate and the group should work on the next data source in their indicator category. The lead for each data source is responsible for recording the data quality information about that data source. In addition, the group should identify a timekeeper to make sure that all of the data sources are examined in the time allotted. You and the critical friend (if present) should circulate to provide differential support, critique, and encouragement as needed.

Bring the whole group back together and conduct a 15- to 20-minute whole-group discussion about the process and the results.

Identify an individual who will collect all the information about data quality from the leads, compile it into a single electronic file, and distribute the file to all the participants within a week.

> *Journal Writing*
>
> Reflect on the data quality activity and question. How do you use data in your work?

Segment 5: How Do You Make Sense of the Data?

This segment is about making sense of the data in relation to the questions of import already established in the previous segment. It is important to understand the data in context. Using the tacit knowledge of people in the school to collaboratively consider the data is important to make sense of it and better understand the school.

Chapter 5. Becoming Data Literate

Discussion Questions

1. How do you interpret data to make them meaningful information?
2. What are the steps you take to use data to challenge and con firm current knowledge about the school?

Activities

● *First Strokes: Interpreting the Individual Data Sources*

Time: Data preparation, plus 60–90 minutes per data set

Materials: Prepared data, copies of Task Sheet #11 (page 122 of the book *Leading Schools in a Data-Rich World* by Lorna M. Earl and Steven Katz), pens, and copies of Interpreting the Individual Data Sources Activity Sheet (Handout 9)

Prior to this activity, identify individual participants to prepare data presentations of a collected data source. It may be a good idea to maintain continuity by asking participants who were responsible for accessing a given data source in the previous activity to present on those data for this activity. The data presentations should include:

1. A succinct description of the data source, using the results of the data quality activities
2. A key that contains the description of all the variables in the data source
3. Appropriate descriptive statistics of the data (e.g., sample size, missing data, mean, median, mode, frequency table, and frequency graph)
4. Descriptions of how the data were grouped (e.g., by gender, by cohort, by year, by grade level, and by program)
5. Appropriate tables and/or graphs of the data by relevant grouping

Tell the presenters that they are responsible for bringing the data in a presentable format, but they are not necessarily responsible for compiling the data. They can access support from a consultant or internal resource staff for technical expertise as needed.

Organize the participants into groups of three or four based on their interest in the questions developed when blocking the canvas. Tell the groups to have a 5-minute discussion and recollect how data were supposed to help answer the question of interest.

Give the participants who prepared the data a chance to present the documentation they prepared to their group and answer any questions from their group. Give the participants 15 minutes to individually and silently read over the data.

Give the groups 45–70 minutes to examine the data and consider all the questions on Task Sheet #11 except for the last one. Identify a recorder in each group to keep running notes on the group's interpretations using the Interpreting the Individual Data Sources Activity Sheet (Handout 9). Make a point of highlighting the importance of discussing inconsistent interpretations of the common data and of considering other data that would help elucidate the interpretation.

Journal Writing

Reflect on the interpretation discussion you had in your small group. What surprised you about the data, the interpretations, and the discussion?

Make a prediction of what will change about what you think about the school during the collective data interpretation in the next activity.

● *First Strokes: Constructing a Concept Map From Data Interpretations*

Time: 90 minutes

Materials: Copies of completed Interpreting the Individual Data Sources Activity Sheet (Handout 9), copies of Task Sheet #11 (page 122 of the book *Leading Schools in a Data-Rich World* by Lorna M. Earl and Steven Katz), pens, chart paper, and markers

Give the participants 15 minutes to review the activity sheets from the previous activity that their group completed. Post several pieces of chart paper adjacent to each other on the front wall. In one corner, use a marker to visibly write out the priority for the group established in the initial activities.

Conduct a *facilitated response cycle* exercise. Give each group 10 minutes to summarize the questions their data were addressing and the interpretations they developed in the last session. Pick a group and give those participants 10 minutes to present their summary to the rest of the participants. Give the listening participants 10 minutes to respond to the interpretations using the evidence and interpretations they came up with for their indicator categories. Pick a second group to present their summary, and continue the 10-minute presentation and 10-minute response cycle until all the groups have had a chance to present their summary.

After all groups have gone through the presentation-response cycle, facilitate a whole-group debriefing discussion on the relationships between the interpretations of the individual data sources. During this discussion, you should be compiling all of the interpretations from all the data sources together in a concept map on the chart paper at the front of the room. Encourage the group to look for relationships across the questions, data, and interpretations and revisit the priority to develop the concept map. At the end of the session, identify a recorder who will copy the concept map in electronic form and distribute it to all the participants within a week.

Option. In the first activity, the participants were asked to share their perceptions of their school. If time permits, or if the dynamics of the group are such that the commitment to the process is untenable, then repeat the first activity. This time, discuss the differences between the initial perceptions and the current perceptions based on the data collected.

Chapter 6. Creating a Culture of Inquiry

Notes for Facilitators

- Creating a culture of inquiry involves engaging the team to grow the image and display the picture. These are the last two phases in the process of making data-informed decisions that foster a way of thinking and of interacting that makes collaborative inquiry and responsive school improvement changes a regular part of work.

- *The image grows* is the first stage in creating a culture of inquiry. In most cases, when data are examined, instead of answers, more-refined questions are raised. As the team pursues these new questions, the additional information and interpretations need to be incorporated with care in an iterative process that keeps people focused and moving forward with purpose.

- The team should engage in a dialogue where different assumptions and perspectives surface to build collective insight into the picture of the school, and to figure out what are the most appropriate actions to work toward a preferred future picture.

- As the image grows, it is important to *display the picture* and engage other audiences. This stage in the process compels the team to strategically share their learning and engage with other audiences. These accountability conversations build broader support for a culture of inquiry.

Discussion Questions

1. When you have information about your school, how do you interact with people who have a different point of view to build a collective picture of your school?
2. When you are building a collective understanding of your school picture, to what extent are you open to new interpretations that could change your mind?
3. What are some examples of things you do in your school that support a culture of inquiry?

Activity

● *The Image Grows: Consensus About Interpretations*

Time: 210–240 minutes

Materials: Copies of Task Sheet #12 (page 123 of the book *Leading Schools in a Data-Rich World* by Lorna M. Earl and Steven Katz), copies of the concept map from the previous activity (*First Strokes: Constructing a Concept Map From Data Interpretations*), Consensus About Interpretations Activity Sheet (Handout 10), chart paper, markers, and sticky index cards

This activity requires a facilitator who is knowledgeable, trusted, emotionally intelligent, and neutral. The conversations can be emotionally charged. The facilitator needs to keep the team on task, the discussions respectful, and ensure that all voices are welcomed, including voices of dissent. The facilitator will be the key to creating space for multiple voices in the discussion. Including a critical friend in the conversation could prove beneficial.

Distribute copies of Task Sheet #12 and the concept map from the last activity (*Constructing a Concept Map From Data Interpretations*). Group the participants into pairs. Give the pairs 20–25 minutes to review the concept map and answer the three questions on Task Sheet #12. Ask the pairs to write up to three priority answers on sticky index cards (one priority per card).

Post a blank piece of chart paper at three corners of the room. On each piece of paper, write one of the following titles: "Things We Are Sure About and Need to Act On," "Important Insights That Deserve Attention," and "Areas We Need to Know More About" (see Consensus About Interpretations Activity Sheet, Handout 10). Invite the pairs to place their sticky index cards on the appropriate chart paper.

When all of the participants have placed their index cards on the chart paper, keep the pairs together and group the participants into three groups. Ask each group to move to a corner of the room where the chart papers are posted. Give them 20–25 minutes to organize the index cards and synthesize the information. Tell the group to look for similarities and differences in the insights posted on the chart paper in their corner.

Ask the groups to rotate to the next corner. Tell the participants to silently read through the grouped index cards. Give them 10 minutes at each of the other two corners with chart papers. Invite the participants to jot down notes on their observations (e.g., agreement, disagreement, insights that are repeated in a different category).

Conduct a *rotating listening circle* exercise. Give the group that organized the index cards on "Things We Are Sure About and Need to Act On" 10–15 minutes to discuss their observations given what they noticed on the other chart papers. Ask the other two groups to form a listening circle around the discussion group and silently listen to the inner circle group's discussion. Invite the listening circle to join the discussion and facilitate a 20-minute whole group discussion. Repeat the discussion-listening exercise with the groups that organized "Important Insights That Deserve Attention" and "Areas We Need to Know More About," rotating the listening circles, respectively.

Distribute copies of the Consensus About Interpretations Activity Sheet to all of the groups. Give each group 20–30 minutes to connect the insights from the consensus exercise to the questions that the data were originally intended to help answer. Tell each group to connect the ideas to the original questions and highlight the insights where no consensus was achieved. Identify a recorder in each group to keep a master copy to share with the larger group.

Facilitate a whole-group consensus-building discussion that connects the three documents and focus on the insights for which there is still no agreement. Make sure the discussion continues until the root of the differences in understandings is identified and articulated. If no consensus is achieved, the facilitator may want to call a vote on priorities for action.

When the session comes to a close, ask the participants to reflect on the short-term and medium-term plans they would like to take to the whole staff. Ask one to two participants from each of the groups to form a subcommittee that will develop a skeleton action plan based on the consensus achieved in this activity for the next session.

Segment 6: How Do You Do Something About What You Find?

This segment is about doing something about the collective interpretation of the data. The purpose of the process, until now, was to get some good information about a specific area of concern that was identified as a priority. Now that you have some good information, it is time to make some informed decisions on what to do next. This segment describes a process on how to develop an action plan that includes multiple stakeholders.

Chapter 6. Creating a Culture of Inquiry

Discussion Questions

1. How do you take information and make action-oriented decisions to improve your school?
2. When you want to share your learning with different audiences, to what extent do you differentiate your communication method?

Activities

● *The Image Grows: Moving to Action*

Time: 60 minutes

Materials: Copies of the Consensus About Interpretations Activity Sheet (Handout 10), skeleton action plan, pens, and copies of Task Sheet #13 (page 124 of the book *Leading Schools in a Data-Rich World* by Lorna M. Earl and Steven Katz)

Distribute the copies of the skeleton action plan to all the participants. Give the subcommittee 10–15 minutes to present the plan to the larger group. Ask them to include a brief explanation of how they developed the plan. Invite the group to comment and modify the plan. Facilitate the discussion to develop a set of action items that align with the insights in each of the categories: "Things We Are Sure About and Need to Act On," "Important Insights That Deserve Attention," and "Areas We Need to Know More About."

Give the participants 10 minutes to read pages 101–102, focusing their attention on the Stages in Growth continuum. Ask the participants to individually reflect on their own interests and capacities. Ask the participants to personally answer the following questions:

1. In what areas am I most interested?
2. What am I good at? For what action could I act as an expert contributor?
3. What do I need or want to learn? For what action would I like to be a team member so that I can build those capacities?

Lead a whole-group discussion, going through the actions one at a time and answering the first three questions listed on Task Sheet #13. As the participants discuss their own interests in leading specific actions and on being part of a team for specific actions, ask them to think of other people in the school who would be good contributors for specific actions.

Ask the team leaders to build and work with their team to answer the rest of the questions on Task Sheet #13. Organize a series of regular times over the next month when the team leaders will report back their progress on Task Sheet #13 to the larger group. One of the follow-up sessions needs to be scheduled after the *Displaying the Picture: Sharing the Learning* activity (next activity).

● *Displaying the Picture: Sharing the Learning*

Time: 75 minutes

Materials: Copies of completed Task Sheet #13 (page 124 of the book *Leading Schools in a Data-Rich World* by Lorna M. Earl and Steven Katz), copies of completed Task Sheet #5 (page 115), and copies of Task Sheet #14 (page 125), chart paper, markers, and pens

Give the participants 10–15 minutes to read pages 97–98 in the book. Tell them to think about how they recognize these practices in their schools, and to what extent they believe these practices exist in their school. Organize the participants into groups of three and give them 10 minutes to discuss their reactions to the guidelines.

Lead a series of whole-group *brainstorming* exercises to further develop communication possibilities with multiple audiences.

Post a chart paper at the front of the room and title it "What We Do Now." Lead a brainstorming session to identify all of the ways in which participants currently communicate with their community. Record the responses on the chart paper at the front of the room.

Ask the participants to review their completed Task Sheet #5 where they recorded the identified audiences. Give them 10–15 minutes to discuss whether the current methods listed on the chart paper reach all the intended audiences on their lists.

Post a chart paper adjacent to the one in the front of the room. Lead a brainstorming session on how the current communication methods can be used to share what they are doing. Record the responses on the blank chart paper so that the new ideas are appropriately aligned to those on the first chart paper.

Post another chart paper on the front wall adjacent to the others and title it "What Else We Can Do." Lead a brainstorming session on alternative ways of engaging audiences. Record the new ideas on the chart paper.

Give the participants 5–10 minutes to silently review the series of three chart papers containing the responses from the brainstorming sessions. Ask them to individually consider whether all the intended audiences would be reached using the listed current and new communication methods. If they think that there are identified audiences that would not be affected by the communication methods, then ask them to work in groups of four to develop targeted communication methods for those specific audiences.

Group the participants by their "action" groups. Give the groups 20 minutes to use the ideas from this activity to build the skeleton for a communication strategy for their action. Ask the groups to complete the last question on Task Sheet #14 and develop their communication strategy as they continue to work on their action plans.

Journal Writing

Reflect on the whole process to date of using data for decision making. What is the most valuable thing you learned? How has it affected how you see your school and your professional work?

Segment 7: Sustaining the Process

This segment is about remembering that the first cycle is only the beginning. The process is iterative and never ending. There needs to be a drive to constantly improve schools and the process by which we improve schools. Sustaining the cycle of inquiry requires determination, interest, caring, and a commitment to build capacity and make improvement a priority. This segment reminds you that there is always a next step.

Chapter 7. Sustaining the Process: The Cycle of Inquiry

Notes for Facilitators

- It is important to target your energies where they will be productive, because the effort in using data to improve schools is substantial.

- The challenge for maintaining the cycle of inquiry is to embed and sustain the capacities for using data wisely. Creating a safe learning space for individuals to move from novice to proficient in a practical way that benefits the school requires sensitivity and determination from school leaders.

- Routinely having respectful accountability conversations with multiple audiences in the school fosters the cycle of inquiry and keeps in mind that school improvement is a living process.

Discussion Questions

1. What are the practical things that you can do to sustain the cycle of inquiry in your school?
2. How will you enhance your school's engagement in the inquiry process for the next cycle?

Handouts

Handout 1. Metaphor Reflection Activity Sheet

Setting the Canvas	Planning This Picture	Blocking the Canvas	The First Strokes	The Image Grows	Displaying the Picture
• What is our purpose?	• What do we *think* we know?	• What do we want (or need) to know?	• How do we make sense of this?	• What does this picture include?	• How will we engage the audience?
• What roles do we play?	• Where do we want to go?	• What data do we need?	• What does it all mean?	• What will we do as a result of our new knowledge?	• How will we share what we have learned?
• Who are the audiences?		• How good are these data?			

43

Handout 2. Initial Environmental Scan Activity Sheet: Part 1

Priority: _____

Group Membership: _____

_____

_____

_____

_____

_____

Important Factor Related to Priority Area	What Do You Already Know?	What Data Inform You?	How Could You Find Out More?	Who Will Find Out More?

Handout 3. Initial Environmental Scan Activity Sheet: Part 2

Important Factor Related to Priority Area	Probable Future	Preferred Future	Extent of Gap Between Probable and Preferred Future

Handout 4. Selecting Your Colors Activity Sheet

Indicator Category	Current Information *What do you already know about the indicator category in relation to your priority? (Existing data and tacit knowledge)*	Additional Information
Student/Community Demographics		
Student Achievement		
Teaching and Assessment Practices		
Parental Opinion and Behaviors		
School Culture		
Student Attitudes		
Staff Characteristics		
Programs		
Resources and Materials		
Physical Plant		
Professional Development		
Other		

Handout 5. Blocking the Canvas: From Indicator Categories to Questions Activity Sheet

Indicator Category	Current Information *What do you already know about the indicator category in relation to your priority? (Existing data and tacit knowledge)*	Questions
Student/Community Demographics		
Student Achievement		
Teaching and Assessment Practices		
Parental Opinion and Behaviors		
School Culture	*This column will have the ideas from the previous activity.*	*This column is where the participants will turn their conjectures and hypotheses from the last activity into questions that can be investigated*
Student Attitudes		
Staff Characteristics		
Programs		
Resources and Materials		
Physical Plant		
Professional Development		
Other		

Handout 6. Blocking the Canvas: From Questions to Data Sources Activity Sheet

Indicator Category: _____

Group Membership: _____

Questions	Data Types	Data Sources	Access Procedures _(Including who will do what to access the data and the timelines)_

Handout 7. Data Quality Activity Sheet

Data Quality Characteristics	Descriptions	Where to Access Information From Data Source
Reliability		
Validity		
Reference Points		

Handout 8. Questions About Data Quality Activity Sheet

1. Describe the data located by answering the following questions:

   a. Why were the data collected?

   b. When were the data collected?

   c. How were the data collected?

   d. Who collected the data?

   e. From whom were the data collected (e.g., student, teachers, or parents)?

2. How reliable are the data?

3. How valid are the data?

4. What are the reference points for the data that can be used for interpretation?

5. Do the data give you information about the things you want to understand? Do the data help you answer the question for which you sought it out in the activity "From Questions to Data Sources"?

6. What are your reservations about the data?

7. How much attention does this data source deserve?

Handout 9. Interpreting the Individual Data Sources Activity Sheet

Data Source: _____

Group Membership: _____

Question	Data	Critical Limitation Comment	Interpretation(s)

Handout 10. Consensus About Interpretations Activity Sheet

Questions From the Concept Map	Insights From the Data		Areas We Need to Know More About
	Things We Are Sure About and Need to Act On	Important Insights That Deserve Attention	

Workshop Evaluation Form

- How well did the seminar meet the goals and objectives?

- How will you apply what you learned during this seminar in your daily professional life?

- What professional support will you need to implement what you have learned from this seminar?

- How well did the topics explored in this seminar meet a specific need in your school or district?

- How relevant was this topic to your professional life?

Process

- How well did the instructional techniques and activities facilitate your understanding of the topic?

- How can you incorporate the activities learned today into your daily professional life?

- Were a variety of learning experiences included in the seminar?

- Was any particular activity memorable? What made it stand out?

Context

- Were the facilities conducive to learning?

- Were the accommodations adequate for the activities involved?

Overall

- Overall, how successful would you consider this seminar? Please include a brief comment or explanation.

- What was the most valuable thing you gained from this seminar experience?

Additional Comments

SOURCE: Adapted from *Evaluating Professional Development* by Thomas R. Guskey, Corwin Press, 2000.

Notes

CORWIN PRESS

The Corwin Press logo—a raven striding across an open book—represents the union of courage and learning. Corwin Press is committed to improving education for all learners by publishing books and other professional development resources for those serving the field of PreK–12 education. By providing practical, hands-on materials, Corwin Press continues to carry out the promise of its motto: **"Helping Educators Do Their Work Better."**